DE SPECULATIONE MUSICAE

MUSICOLOGICAL STUDIES & DOCUMENTS

ARMEN CARAPETYAN
General Editor

A TRANSLATION OF

PART VI

OF

WALTER ODINGTON'S

DE SPECULATIONE MUSICAE

AMERICAN INSTITUTE OF MUSICOLOGY

MUSICOLOGICAL STUDIES & DOCUMENTS

31

WALTER ODINGTON

DE SPECULATIONE MUSICAE

PART VI

Translated by

JAY A. HUFF

AMERICAN INSTITUTE OF MUSICOLOGY

1973

INTRODUCTION

Collectively, the medieval treatises on music make available two essentially different kinds of information. On the one hand, we have the *practical,* i.e., information that a contemporary musician, as artist, would presumably have found useful; and on the other hand, the *abstract* or "speculative" (basically a recapitulation of ancient Greek theory as transmitted to the Middle Ages by Boethius), information that only the more scientifically minded would have been concerned with. The two kinds often appear in the same treatise, as they do in the *De speculatione musicae* of Walter Odington (*fl. intra ca.* 1280-1320), a monk of Evesham Abbey near Worcester, England. However, as its title suggests, Odington's work is heavily weighted in favor of the speculative. Only the last two of its six parts deal with "practical" matters. In the earlier sections, Odington treats of such things as numerical proportions, the application of those proportions to the determination of the sizes of intervals, divisions of the monochord, and so on. Furthermore, part V, though certainly of practical import, being in essence a tonary or theoretical guide to plainsong, still presents merely conventional material within the purview of its subject. It is only in part VI that we get something substantial that is not also obtainable from other sources. This last section, though less than satisfactory for many reasons, nevertheless contains the only contemporaneous discussion of English mensural polyphony in the late thirteenth and early fourteenth centuries that we have.*

* The content of *De speculatione musicae* is discussed at length in *The Summa de Speculatione Musicae of Walter Odington: A Critical Edition and Commentary* by Frederick Fisher Hammond (University Microfilms, 1965).

A critical edition of the full text of *De speculatione musicae* by F. F. Hammond is published as No. 14 in the series *Corpus Scriptorum de Musica* of the American Institute of Musicology.

Now, the foregoing remarks should not be taken to mean that the content of the other five parts of the work is not of sufficient significance to justify an English translation of the entire treatise eventually. If there were no other reason (and there are others), the very scope of Odington's extensive *summa* warrants its being made accessible to readers of English some day. However, the overriding importance of part VI, plus the fact that the state of the manuscripts renders interpretation of many passages in the earlier sections highly problematical, are offered here as justifications for a separate translation of part VI at this time.*

J. A. H.
The Ohio State University

* This work was supported, in part, by The Ohio State University Development Fund through its Faculty Fellowship Program. I also wish to acknowledge the generous assistance of Dr. Frederick Hammond of the University of California at Los Angeles.

A TRANSLATION OF PART VI OF WALTER ODINGTON'S *DE SPECULATIONE MUSICAE*

[Here] begins the sixth and last part. It has 18 *capitula*: Longs, breves, and semibreves — Plicas — The various ways in which the long is said to be perfected and imperfected — The various ways in which the breve is said to be true (*recta*) or altered — Rests — The modes used in part-music — The perfection and imperfection of modes, and mutation [of mode] — Ligatures — Ligature values — How each mode is to be notated in ligatures — Types of part-music — On the composition of organum [part-music], and of pure organum first — The rondellus — The conductus — The copula — The motet — The hocket — On the [proper] manner of singing [pure organum].

Longs, breves, and semibreves

We have finished with simple harmony [monophonic music]. It remains now to explain multiple harmony [part-music], which I call *diaphony*. Diaphony is a consonance-dissonance (*concors discordia*) of lower parts with higher; and it is said to be this because, rather than moving by consonances throughout, a subsequent consonance is used to alleviate the harsh effect of a preceding dissonance. And this is the sort of composition commonly called *organum*. In this part, then, there are three things of significance, namely: consonance and the consonant intervals, discussed already; unequal time values in verse, also discussed; and inequality of values in combined voice-parts as indicated in notation, and this is the subject of what follows. For when all of these elements come together in the same piece, the ear is refreshed with a marvelous sweetness.

So, then, inequality of time values results when one note moves slower, another quicker. The slow one, which used to be named *virga*, is now called a *long*. It is a square note with a stem on the right, thus: . But the quick one, which used to be named punctus, is now called a *breve*, a square figure, thus:

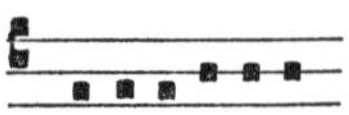 .

Now, among earlier composers of organum the long had two tempora as it does in verse meters, but later it was brought to perfection; that is, it was given the value of three tempora in the likeness of the Blessed Trinity, which is the highest perfection.[1] Thus a long of this type is called perfect, whereas that which has only two tempora is said to be imperfect. There is

The following abbreviations are used in the notes:

CS: Coussemaker, Edmond de. *Scriptorum de musica medii aevi nova series.* 4 vols. Paris, 1864-76.

HS: Hammond, Frederick Fisher. *The Summa de Speculatione Musicae of Walter Odington: A Critical Edition and Commentary.* University Microfilms, Inc. Ann Arbor, 1965.

HM: *Hieronymus de Moravia: Tractatus de musica.* Ed. Simon M. Cserba. Regensburg, 1935.

MD: *Musica Disciplina.* 1948-

MTT: Dittmer, Luther. *Musical Theorists in Translation,* Vols. I & II. Institute of Mediaeval Music, Ltd. Brooklyn, n.d.

WO: *Walter Odington: De speculatione musicae.* Ed. Frederick Fisher Hammond. *Corpus Scriptorum de Musica* 14, American Institute of Musicology, 1970.

The following books and articles are referred to by surname of author only:

Apel, Willi. *The Notation of Polyphonic Music 900-1600.* 5th edition. Cambridge, 1953.

Sanders, Ernest. "Binary Rhythm and Alternate Third Mode in the 13th and 14th Centuries." *Journal of the American Musicological Society,* XV (1962), 249-291.

Strunk, Oliver. *Source Readings in Music History.* New York, 1950.

Wolf, Johannes. *Geschichte der Mensural-Notation von 1250-1460.* Leipzig, 1904.

"Manuscript" here indicates the one codex in which the whole of Odington's *De speculatione musicae* is contained, MS 410 of the library of Corpus Christi College, Cambridge.

[1] For various interpretations of this controversial sentence see HS, pp. 86-87; Sanders, *art. cit.*; Dittmer, "Binary Rhythm, Musical Theory, and the Worcester Fragments," MD, VII (1953), 39-57; and J. Handschin, "The Summer Canon and its Background," MD, III (1949), 55-94, and V, 65-113.

still another kind, called *double long*, with the value of two perfect longs; and that value is expressed with a single figure to avoid breaking up a plainchant tenor, thus: 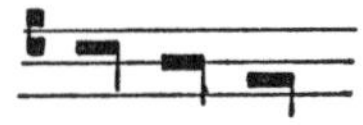. Hence a perfect long can be resolved into three breves, any one of which is called a true breve (*recta brevis*) because any is true in respect to another, *true* being sometimes used for *equal.* But if it is resolved into only two breves, the first will be called true, the second altered (*altera*); [but notated] thus: 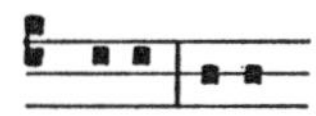

 because the one sign does for the altered breve also. It has the value of an imperfect long. The breve, moreover, was formerly resolved into two semibreves, which are named for that fact; but nowadays it is resolved sometimes into two, sometimes into three. When it is resolved into two, the first semibreve is called *minor*, the second *major* because it contains two minor.

The notation for these values derives from types of quadrangle: One is a square; [i.e.] it has equal sides and angles; such are the longs and breves. The other has equal sides and unequal angles, thus: . And the latter is the notation for semibreves.

The breve is divisible still further, into six or seven parts, which, however, are still called semibreves, though with less justification. But because a continuum can be divided infinitely, and time is a continuum, and because notes are measured in units of time, notes will therefore be infinitely divisible. Thus, just as a long is divided into breves, and breves into semibreves, so I divide semibreves basically into three parts, which I call *minutae*, although I notate them as semibreves in order not to appear to differ from other musicians. And when a breve that has been divided into two semibreves follows one divided into three, or vice versa — the second divided into three, the first into two — I place the *divisio* [i.e., *punctus divisionis*] thus:

 . But when the breve is di-

vided into four, five, or more parts, it will not be marked with the aforesaid divisio but with a little circle like this, which is also a sign of division, thus: [2]  .

Then, of the [first] four notes the first two are minor semibreves, the last two *minutae*, meaning smallest or quickest; and the same applies to the others.

Plicas

The plica consists of a tone and the inflexion of that tone, written with a single sign. Only longs and breves are subject to the plica. One type of plica ascends, the other descends. They correspond respectively to the *semitonus* and *semivocalis* in plainchant. The descending long plica has the longer stem on the right, thus:  . The [descending] breve plica is

[2] Wolf suggests the following values for these groups (p. 22):

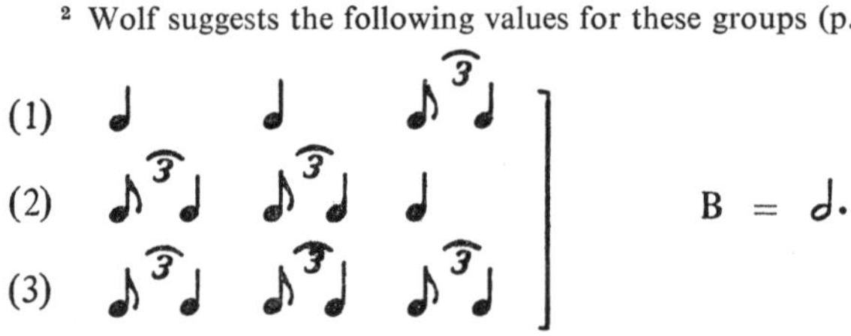

Sanders, discussing Rules VII and VIII of the fourth rubric in the *Regulae* of Robert of Handlo (CS I, 388a f.; and MTT, II, 14-16), recommends an even division of the breve when resolved into four semibreves (p. 253), adding (n. 13), "This also agrees essentially with Walter Odington..." We are not told the basis of this claim, however. Apel denies the possibility of any differentiation of values within groups of four or more semibreves at the putative *tempo giusto* of Ars Antiqua, B = MM. 60-70 (p. 324), implying an even division of all such groups. Yet, as a matter of fact, it is not only possible but not even very difficult to sing at least the first of the above groups at such a tempo, as anyone can determine for himself simply by trying it. Moreover, an even division of group 1, at any rate, is excluded by Odington's explanation, which for once is quite unambiguous: The first two notes are minor semibreves, a value he has just defined as 1/3 breve. The result can only be what Wolf suggests, or: 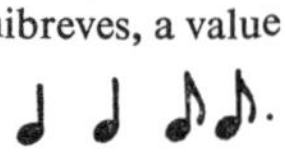. As for groups 2 and 3, an even division here is of course more likely, for the reason Apel gives. However, the phrase "et sic de aliis" ("and the same applies to the others"), with which the next sentence ends, implies that the last two groups are divided similarly to the first. If there was an uneven division, then, it is possible that the larger values were placed at the beginning, not at the end, of the groups of shorter values as of the longer. In that event the example would not of course be the basis of later practice as Wolf and Sanders suppose.

the opposite, with the [longer] stem on the left, thus:  The ascending long plica also has the longer stem on the right, thus: 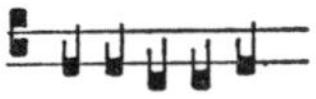. It is also found sometimes with only one stem, thus: . The ascending breve plica has the longer stem on the left, thus:[3] 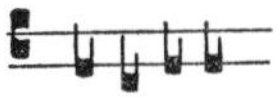 .

The various ways in which a long is said to be perfected and imperfected

A long is perfected when it precedes another long, thus: 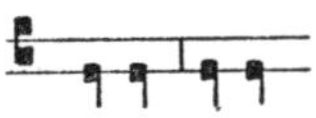 or when given the sign of perfection, thus: 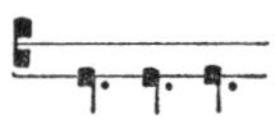 or when it is followed by two breves, thus:   or three, thus: 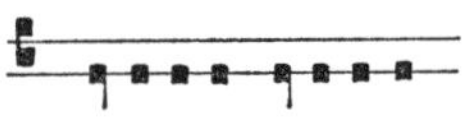  unless the first [breve] and the following are divided off thus: 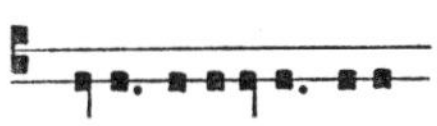  or a breve precedes the long, thus: 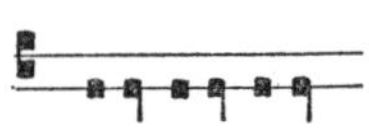  in which cases the long is imperfected. It is also imperfected when followed by a single breve, thus: 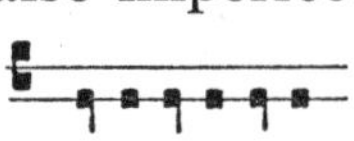 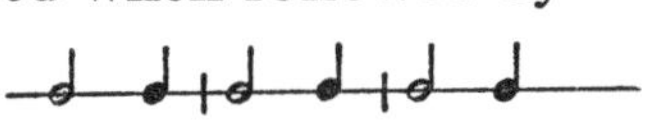 or four or more, thus:[4]

[3] The assignment of time values to the subdivisions of plicated notes at this period presumably accords with the rules given by Magister Lambert (CS, I, 273; see also Apel. pp. 227 & 298). An even division of the plicated imperfect long seems to be indirectly confirmed by Odington at the end of cap. 10 (q.v.) where he mentions the practice of notating mode 6 in binary ligature with propriety and perfection plicated.

[4] The example appears thus in the manuscript:

That the *punctus divisionis* should be taken rather as a fifth breve is indicated both by the superfluity of a division sign here and by the fact that "vel plures" of the phrase "quatuor vel plures" ("four or more") in the preceding sentence is not otherwise illustrated by the examplee.

 or by the value of a breve resolved into semibreves, thus:[5] 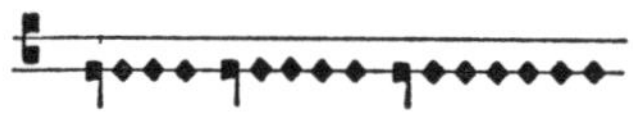

The various ways in which the breve is said to be true (recta) or altered

When two breves follow a long and precede another long, the first breve is said to be true and the second altered, thus:  unless the breves are divided off thus:[6] 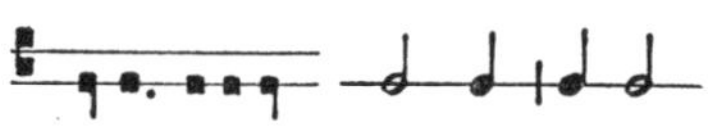 in which case both are true. And similarly if two breves precede a long, the second is said to be altered, thus: 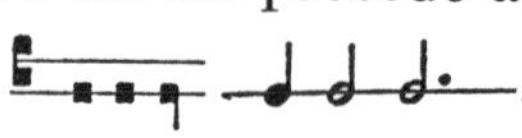. But if there are several breves, all are true unless a dot or stroke of division separates the last two from the others, in which case the last is said to be altered, thus: . But if there are three breves between two longs, all are true, thus: 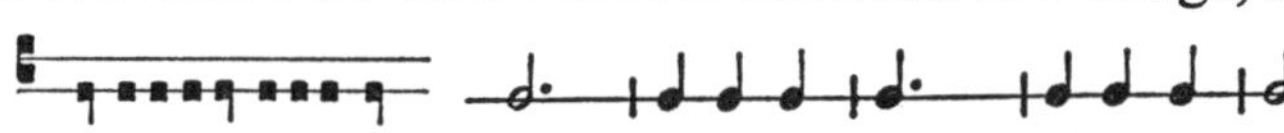 unless a dot of division happens to be placed between the first and the two following, thus:  in which case the first imperfects the first long, while the first of the remaining breves is true, the second altered.

Rests

Rests are certain periods of silence for the voices such that, while one person is singing, another is silent. Accordingly, signs

[5] The values of the semibreves in the second and third groups of the example are presumably equivalent to those in the first and third groups of the example discussed in note 2.

[6] MS:  .

are provided for these periods [of silence] in the parts, namely bars intersecting the lines of the staff. Thus the rest for a perfect long occupies three spaces and touches four lines. The rest for an imperfect long occupies two spaces, and the same applies to the rest for an altered breve. The rest for a [*recta*] breve occupies one space, and that for a semibreve, half of one space. When all voices rest at the same time, a bar is drawn through the whole staff, and this is referred to as "the end of a section"[7] Thus:[8]

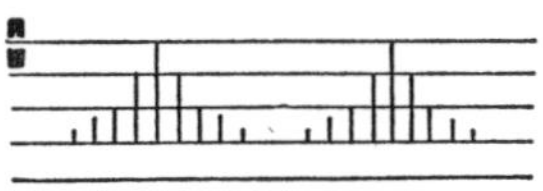 .

Also, when a breve or a long precedes a long or breve rest, they are reckoned as though the omitted long or breve were present. Thus, just as a long before another long is perfect, so it is perfect before a long rest; and the same applies to the other values.

The modes used in part-music

Mode in this part means a succession of longs and breves in fixed order. For example, when the unit is long-plus-breve, the part is said to be in the first mode, thus:  . The second mode is the opposite, thus:  . The third proceeds by a long and two breves, thus: 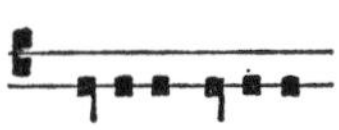 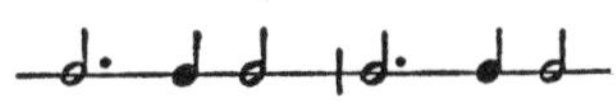. The fourth is the opposite, thus:  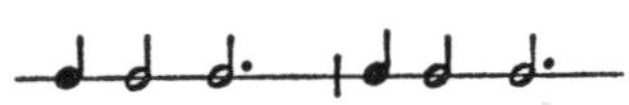 The fifth moves entirely in longs, thus:  . The sixth consists entirely of breves and semibreves, thus:

[7] The phrase "finis punctorum," here rendered "the end of a section," is translated in Strunk as "double bar" (p. 149 *et passim*).

[8] The example seems to have been taken directly from Franco (HM, p. 245; Strunk, p. 150) since it includes the minor semibreve rest, which Odington does not mention in the text.

There are also other, secondary modes as, for example, when a part moves by long-plus-breve followed by breve-plus-long, with a modal *divisio* between the breves, thus: 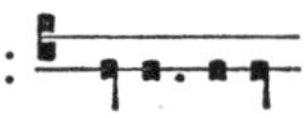 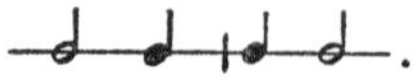. But this mode is a combination of the first and the second and is reduced to one or the other of them. The same is true when a part moves by a breve and a long followed by two breves and a long, thus:  this being a combination of the third and the fourth. And so on for the various other possibilities.

The order of the modes, incidentally, was determined by the order in which they were invented and used.[9]

The perfection and imperfection of modes, and their mutation

The above modes have [three perfect and] three imperfect forms,[10] I submit, and I shall pair each of them with verse feet to show which metrical feet are appropriate to which forms.

The first perfect form of mode 1 is thus: 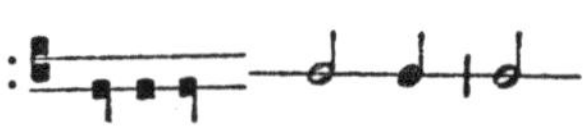 suitable for amphimacer. The second is this: 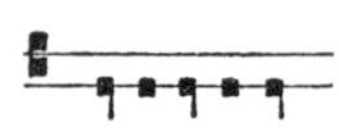  suitable for a trochee plus an amphimacer. The third [perfect form] of mode 1 is this: 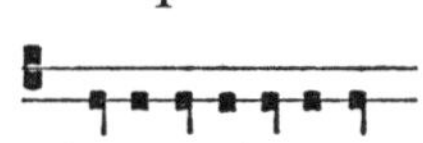  the same as a ditrochee plus an amphimacer. And for these the proper rest is the true breve.

[9] Cf. Sanders, *art. cit.*, esp. pp. 278-287.

[10] Throughout this section Odington uses the word *modus* indiscriminately for either "mode" or "ordo," in the usual senses of these terms. (The same can be said of *ordines* in the last sentence of chapter 7, q.v., where plainly it has the meaning "orders of values" and hence "modes.") Although it is generally apparent from the context which meaning is to be assigned to *modus*, for the sake of greater clarity the word is here translated otherwise that "mode" when it means "ordo."

The first imperfect form of mode 1 is this: 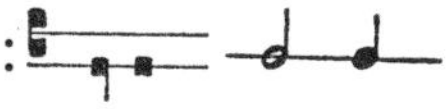
suitable for the trochee. The second is this: 
 which is for the ditrochee. The third imperfect form of mode 1 is this:  the same as an amphimacer plus an amphibrach. And for these the proper rest is an imperfect long and a true breve, thus: .

The first perfect form of mode 2 is this: 
like the amphibrach. The second is this: 
 suitable for an iamb plus an amphibrach. The third is this: 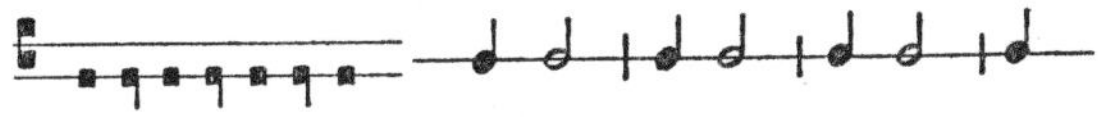 equal to a diiamb plus an amphibrach. And the proper rest for these is the imperfect long, thus:[11]  .

The first imperfect form of mode 2 is this: 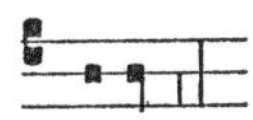
 like the iamb. The second is this: 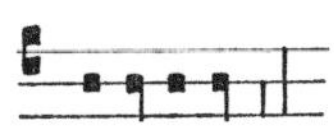
 suitable for a diiamb. The third is this:  suitable for an iamb plus a diiamb. The proper rest for these forms is a true breve and an imperfect long, thus: .

This mode often changes to the first imperfect with the

[11] The example is corrected from the manuscript, in which it is exactly the same as the one that follows.

omission of the long rest, and the first [changes to the second] imperfect with the removal of the breve rest.[12]

The first form of mode 3 perfect is this: 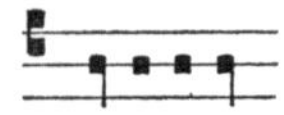

[12] Cf. Franco (HM, p. 245; Strunk, p. 150). If the words "iste modus" are presumed to refer to the mode just described, that is, the imperfect form of mode 2, then Odington must mean that the rest omitted from an ordo of this mode is replaced by a note of the same value and that this note then becomes the first of an ordo in the new mode, thus:

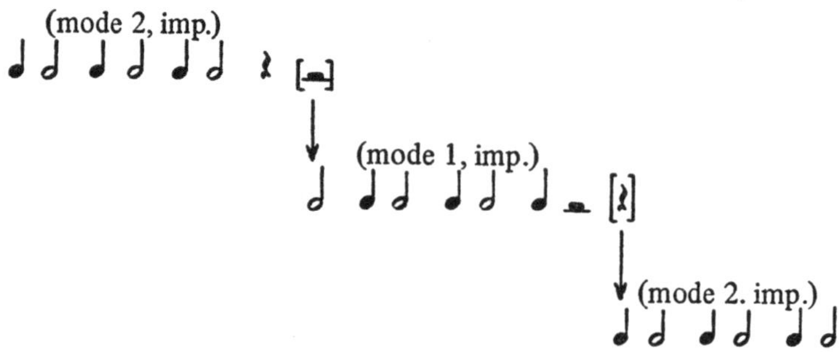

It will be noted that Franco's description is based on the opposite relation of note and rest; i.e., an omitted note is replaced by the same value in rests. However, the result is the same because Franco starts with the perfect form of the initial mode, thus (*locis cit.*):

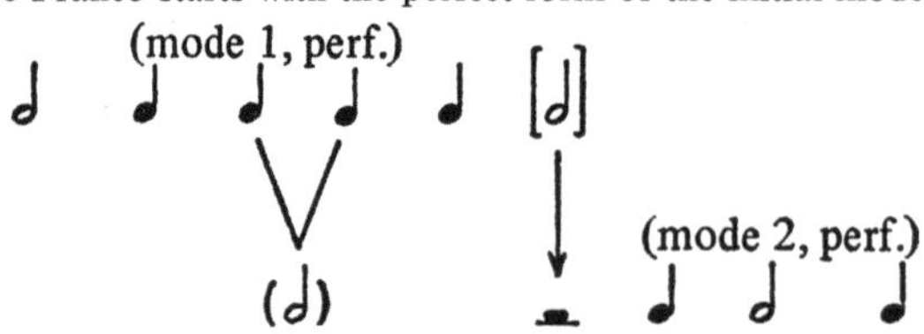

and

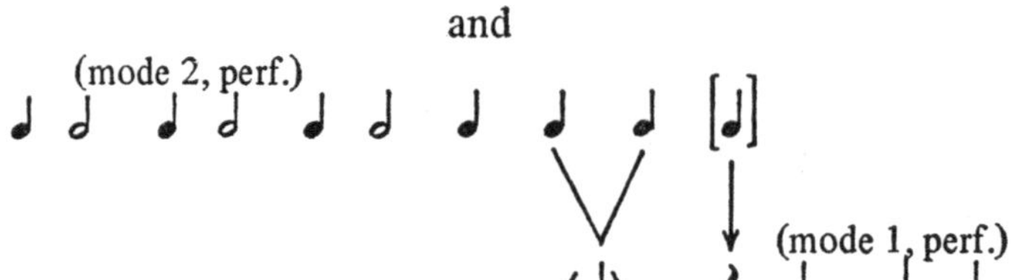

It is probably significant, too, that both here and later in a similar statement about modes 3 and 4 (see n. 14) Odington says explicitly that the new or resultant mode is of the imperfect form. There seems to be no reason for this specification unless Odington is talking about a regular or cyclic alternation of modes such as Anonymous IV describes (CS, I, 329; MTT, I, 11), a situation which requires of course that both modes be, in effect, imperfect.

Finally, it has been questioned whether the examples in Franco actually do represent a change of mode. For any consideration of this subject it is important to keep in mind, as Professor Theodore Karp has pointed out ("Towards a Critical Edition of Notre Dame Organa Dupla," *The Musical Quarterly*, Vol. LII, No. 3, p. 362), that thirteenth-century

It is like the choriamb. The second is this: 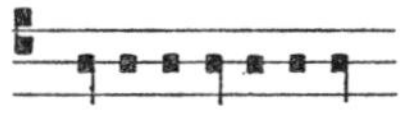
 equivalent to a dactyl plus a choriamb. The third is this: 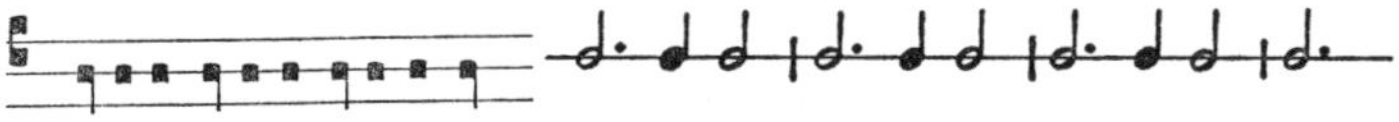
equivalent to two dactyls plus a choriamb. The proper rest for this mode is a true and an altered breve, in other words, a perfect long.

The first form of mode 3 imperfect is this:[13] 
 like a dactyl. The second is like two dactyls:  . The third is this:  equivalent to three dactyls. The proper rest for this mode is a perfect long plus a true and an altered breve, thus:[13] 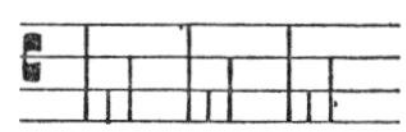

The first form of mode 4 perfect is this, equivalent to an anapaest plus a pyrrhic: 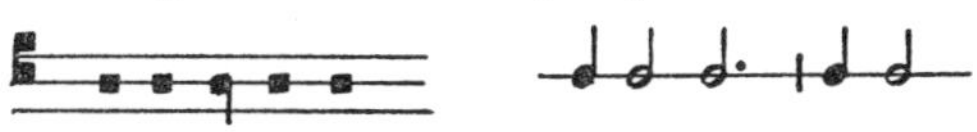 . The second is this:  suitable for two dactyls plus a pyrrhic. The third is this: 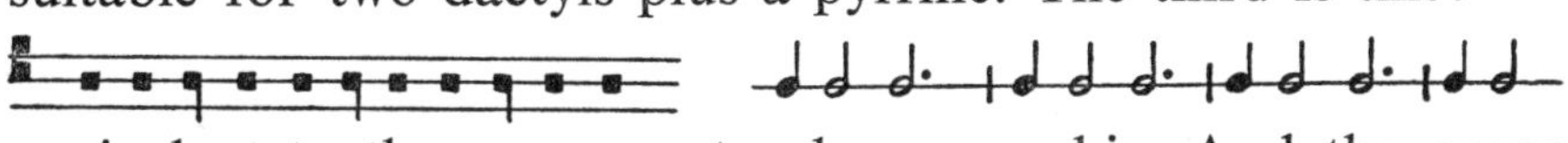 equivalent to three anapaests plus a pyrrhic. And the proper rest in this mode is the perfect long.

theorists commonly held mode to be determined by order of time values within the ordo rather than by placement of stress. (Cf. Anon. IV, CS, I, 328, and MTT, I, 11; and Odington above, ch. 6, first sentence.) Thus Strunk's objection (p. 150, n. 13) that Franco's examples are poorly chosen because they do not really show a change of mode (i.e., shift of stress) is not relevant theoretically, although it may be musically. The question of stress is discussed both by Karp (*loc. cit.*) and by William Waite (*The Rhythm of Twelfth-Century Polyphony*, New Haven, 1954, p. 40 f.), who express opposite opinions on the subject. Karp agrees with Strunk that stress does not shift. Waite seems to think it does. As an alternative to this dichotomy, it may be suggested that in the performance practice of the period stress was probably so subordinate to duration as to render the question of its placement largely academic.

[13] In the manuscript the long rest in this example and in the examples for mode 4 below appears to be imperfect. (See WO, p. 125, *app. crit.* 21-23 & 27-30. See also n. 27 below.)

The first form of mode 4 imperfect is this: 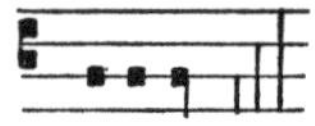  like an anapaest. The second: 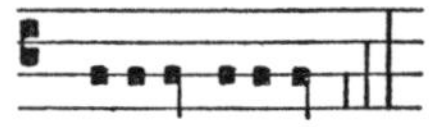  suitable for a double anapaest. The third, thus:   equivalent to a triple anapaest. And the proper rest for this mode is a true and an altered breve plus a perfect long, thus: 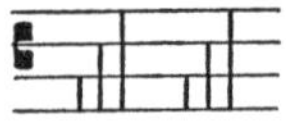  .

This mode changes to the third imperfect if the long rest is taken out, and the third changes to [the fourth], that is, if the two breve rests are removed.[14]

Nor is it improper to have a long of three tempora and an altered breve of two — in the third and fourth modes, that is — even though it was said before [i.e., in part iv] that the long is equal to two tempora in meters of verse; for a long syllable can be stretched as much as need be to make it fit the tone to which it is set. Moreover, not every piece of part-music is written to verse.[15] Another reason it is quite proper to have a long of three tempora and an altered breve of two in modes 3 and 4 is that these modes consist principally of dactyls and anapaests. Now,

[14] Odington seems to be describing a modal shift parallel to the one above involving modes 1 and 2 (see n. 12). If so, the change would presumably be thus:

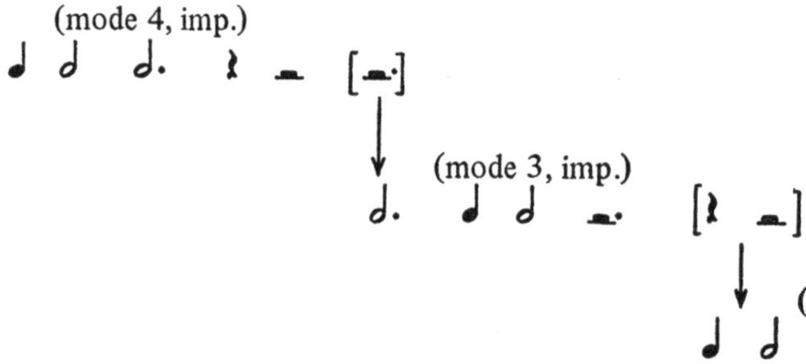

However, Dittmer's assumption that the original mode is perfect leads him to an altogether different interpretation (*art. cit.*, p. 43, n. 4).

[15] The phrase "in carmine," here translated "to verse," is discussed by Dittmer, *art. cit.*, pp. 44-46.

the name "dactyl" derives from the word for finger, *digitus*, and an anapaest is the reverse of a dactyl. The first phalange of the finger is long while the last two are short. The middle one is twice as long as the last, and the first is equivalent to the other two together. Hence this order: breve, altered breve, perfect long, by analogy with the finger. This is why the perfect long originated in modes 3 and 4. Also, it is only in these modes that the breve is altered. Furthermore, it is always the second breve that is altered in both third and fourth modes because, if it were otherwise [i.e., if the first breve were altered], it would clash in combination, unless it just happened to be combined with two rectas. Also, alteration of the first breve would effect a change to mode 1.[16]

The first form of mode 5 [perfect] is this: 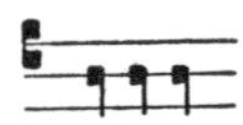  equivalent to the molossus. The second is this: 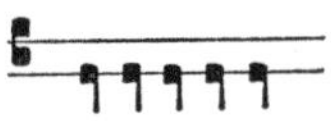  suitable for a molossus plus a spondee. The third is this: 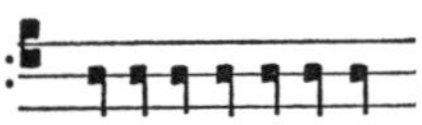  suitable for a molossus plus a dispondee. The rest [in this mode] is the perfect long.

The first form of mode 5 imperfect is this: 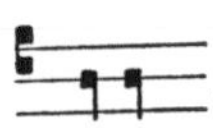  like a spondee. The second is this: 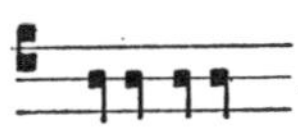  like a dispondee. The third is this: 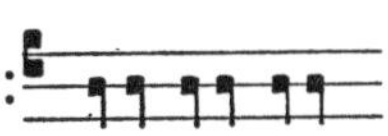 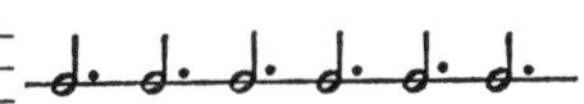 like two molossi. And the rest is that for a [perfect] long. Perfection in this mode, as in the sixth, is considered to depend upon whether a melody in another mode combined with it happens to produce a perfection. Otherwise, the latter series of six longs would be [im]perfect.

The first form of mode 6 perfect runs thus: 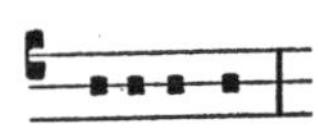  like the proceleusmatic. The second is this:

[16] For other interpretations of this passage see Dittmer, *art. cit.*, p. 43; Sanders, p. 259.

 suitable for a tribrach plus a proceleusmatic. The third is this: 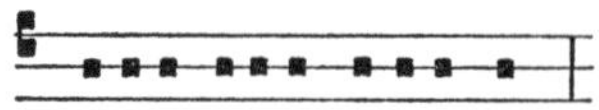  equivalent to a proceleusmatic plus two tribrachs. The rest [in this mode] is the breve.

The first form of mode 6 imperfect is this: 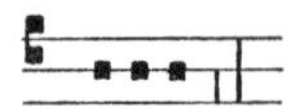  like the tribrach. The second: 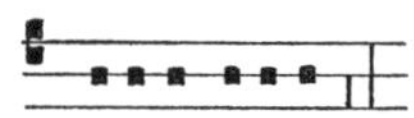  is like a double tribrach. The third:  is suitable for three tribrachs. And the rest [for this mode] is also the breve.

In all modes breves may be resolved into semibreves without changing anything else.

The mode last mentioned is reduced to the second if the imperfect breve rest is replaced by the rest for an imperfect long.[17]

Any other *ordines* besides these may be reduced to the above, and therefore I define only these six, which I have now sufficiently explained.

Ligatures

A ligature is the joining of several notes, because whenever there are notes without text[18] in part-music, they are bound together for the sake of brevity. One kind of ligature ascends,

[17] The reference is evidently to a *reductio modi*:

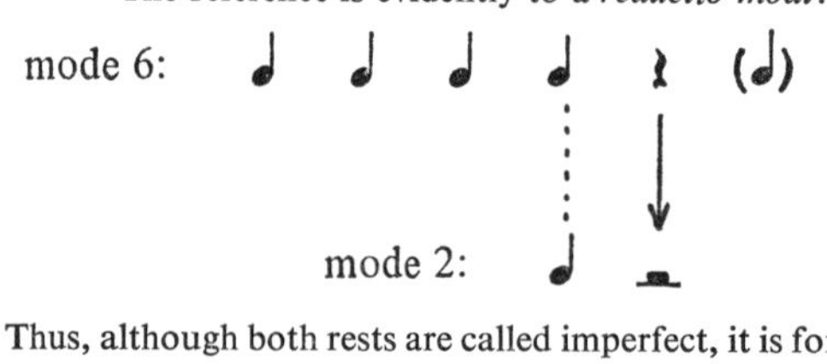

Thus, although both rests are called imperfect, it is for different reasons: The breve is imperfect because it does not complete the foot (see Waite, *op. cit.*, pp. 41-2); the long, because it has the value of two tempora.

[18] I.e., a melisma. See Waite, *op. cit.*, p. 92; Apel, p. 223.

the other descends. An ascending ligature is one whose second note is higher than the first, thus: 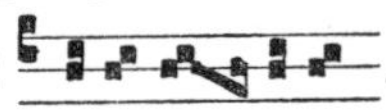. The descending ligature is the opposite thus: . Moreover, a ligature can be with propriety, without propriety, or with opposite propriety; and this is determined by the beginning [i.e., first note] of the ligature. Further, a ligature can be with perfection or without perfection; and this is determined by its end [last note].

A descending ligature, then, is said to be with propriety if it has a stem descending from its first note, thus: 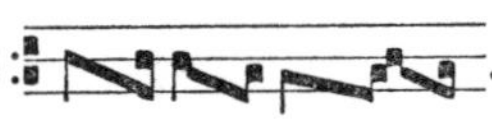. But an ascending ligature is with propriety if it has no stem at all, thus: 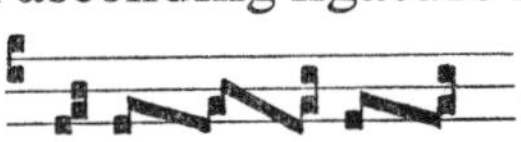. A descending ligature which has no stem is without propriety, thus: . An ascending ligature is without propriety when it has a stem, thus: 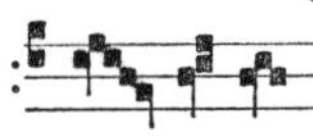. Or thus, according to some: 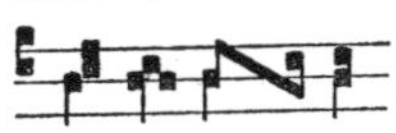. A ligature is with opposite propriety if it has a stem ascending from the first note, whether the ligature itself is ascending or descending, thus:

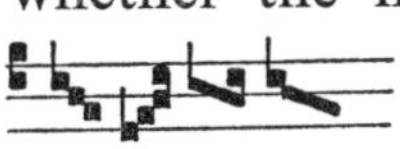

An ascending ligature is with perfection if the penultimate note is directly below the head of the last, like the *pes* or *resupina* in plainsong, thus: 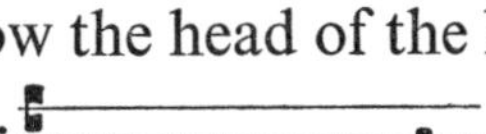. An ascending ligature is said to be without perfection whenever the head of the last note is turned away from the penultimate, thus: 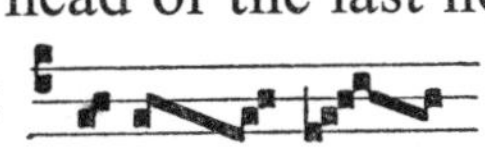 or is part of an oblique stroke, thus: 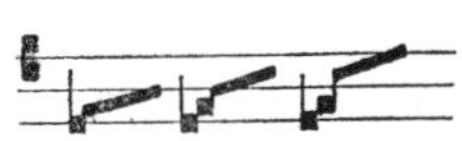. A descending ligature is said to have perfection whenever the last two notes are joined at one corner, the last below [and to the side of] the penultimate, like the *flexa* or *pes flexus*, thus: 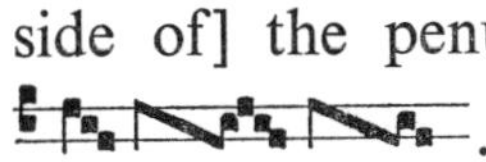. A descending ligature is said to be without perfection when its last two notes are combined in an oblique stroke, thus:  .

Also, a descending ligature with perfection may take the ascending or descending plica, thus: 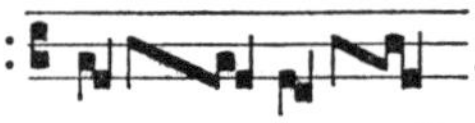. And the same holds if the ligature is without perfection, thus: 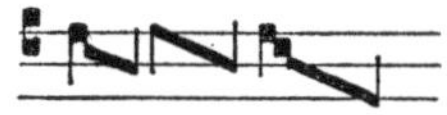

Occasionally an ascending ligature, without perfection, has the plica too; but in this instance the plica, according to some, changes the ligature from imperfect to perfect, thus:

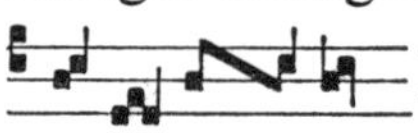 However, the imperfect ascending ligature with oblique stroke remains imperfect even when plicated, thus:

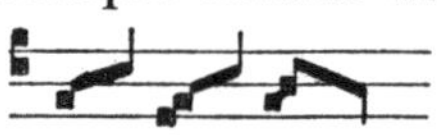 .

Ligature values

Although there are many different opinions regarding the values of ligatures, I shall offer here only the brief rules I myself observe, taking account of the various opposing points of view in the examples that follow.

Every propriety is a breve, every impropriety a long. Opposite propriety results in two semibreves because a single one is not ligated nor are more than two; hence if more [than two] occur, they cannot be grouped together in a single ligature.

Every perfection is a long, imperfection a breve. Moreover, every middle note is a breve except the one that is made a semibreve through opposite propriety.

In ligatures, as in single notes, the long can be both perfect and imperfect, breves both true and altered.

There are other combinations of notes different from the foregoing, but they have to be recognized with the help of these [preceding] and by means of the mode in which they occur. For example:[19] . In the first mode these groups have

[19] For the possible time values in the four anomalous groups that follow, see: for group 1, Apel, p. 333, Dittmer, *art. cit.*, pp. 54-55, Sanders, p. 266; for groups 2 and 3, Apel, pp. 299 & 304; for group 4, Apel, p. 297, HM, p. 244, Strunk, p. 149.

the value of an imperfect long, in the third and fourth, a perfect long. These: , or these: 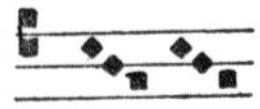 have the value of an imperfect long. These:  are equal to a breve plus a long.

How each mode is to be notated in ligatures

The first mode, according to the rules, begins with a ternary ligature[20] without propriety and with perfection, then proceeds by binary ligatures with propriety and with perfection, thus:  .

Others give the ternary ligature propriety in this mode along with the binary. Consequently, in a *ternaria* the propriety indicates a long, in a *binaria*, a breve, thus:[21] 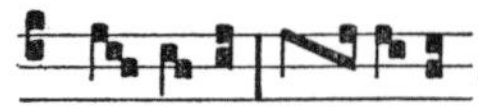. I myself take no account of this practice because it is both improper and contrary to reason. Also they equip the ascending breve with propriety,[22] thus: 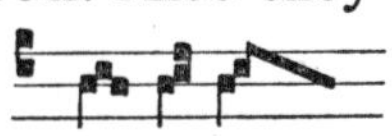 and so they make both propriety and impropriety represent a breve, which is equally improper. Still others notate a long divided into unligated breves in this mode thus:[23] . And they write all

[20] MS: "ternary long" ("ternariam longam").

[21] Odington's objection is evidently based upon the lack of correspondence between the notation as a form and its intended meaning. In the Franconian system the ternary ligature as written here should indicate the values BBL, not LBL, which are of course the values demanded by the mode (see HM, pp. 241-2, and Strunk, pp. 147-8). The theoretical sources for the various pre-Franconian practices to which Odington objects in chapter 9 are noted and discussed by Hammond, pp. 92-95.

[22] I.e., the same in notation, presumably, as one not in propriety. Thus, the second and third ligatures in the example are incorrect by Franco's rules since their initial notes, which the mode requires to be breves, are notated the same way as the inital long of the first ligature.

[23] See HS, pp. 92-93; Sanders, pp. 268-269; Dittmer, *art. cit.*, p. 54. It should be noted that Sanders' version of the second example, , is based on a "correction" of Coussemaker (CS, I, 244a; Sanders, *loc. cit.*, n. 106) and that neither version is that found in the manuscript. However, since the second example is, in the manuscript, almost identical to the first, it is quite possibly an error of the copyist. Certainly Sanders' version is closest to the description given in the text.

semibreves with stems and give them the same shape as breves, thus:[23] 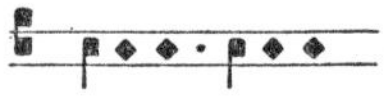. This is quite unsuitable.

The second mode proceeds by binary ligature with propriety and perfection and ends with a single breve, thus:

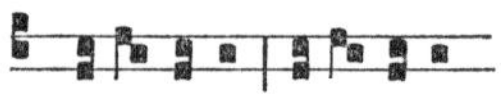 .

In this mode they sometimes ligate a long between two breves; and in a descending ligature they notate this with opposite propriety, thus:  in an ascending ligature, with impropriety,[24] thus:  and always with perfection. Thus at one time they have a perfect ligature ending with a breve, namely the *ternaria*, and at another, one ending with a long, that is, the *binaria*; and this is confusing.

The third mode begins with a four-note ligature without propriety but with perfection; then it proceeds by ternary [ligatures] with both propriety and perfection, thus:[25]

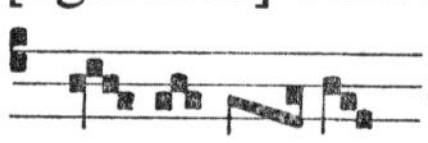. However, if the breves happen to be divided into semibreves, then the first long is not ligated, thus:

 . In fact, there are those who always separate the first long from the following notes and put it by itself, thus: 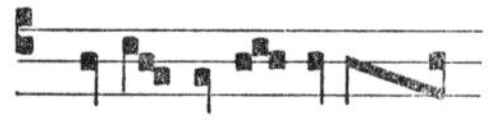 . It is a matter of no great importance; still, since the last note is bound to the others, the first should be too.

The fourth mode proceeds by ternary ligature with propriety and perfection and ends in two breves with propriety and imperfection, thus: 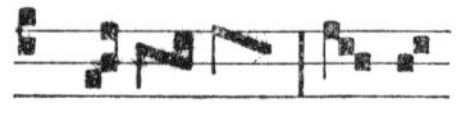.

However, there are those who adopt a procedure, in the

[24] The ascending strokes, indicating of course opposite propriety, not impropriety as stated in the text, may be an erroneous continuation by the scribe of the form shown in the previous example. Also, the last ligature of the former, being ascending, probably belongs here.

[25] The order of time values in this example and in the next three is such that none can be taken as a unit. Evidently, then, each comprises more than one illustration of the point to be made.

third and fourth modes only, which makes it plain that in these modes they divide the long into two breves: The say that a ternary ligature has the value of two longs while a quaternary ligature is equal to a ternary, as a quinary is too,[26] the last [note] being always long unless it follows a binary ligature, in which case they make the last a breve. In a binary ligature, moreover, they make all notes breves, provided a ternary ligature or a long or a long rest follows, thus: 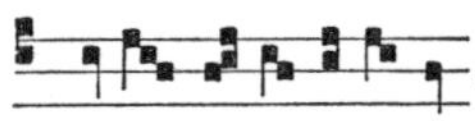. And so perfection is sometimes a breve, sometimes a long. But this mode of identification is ambiguous in any genus, as appears below in cantilenas where there is an admixture of the different rests,[27] because it is not definite what is a breve and what a semibreve inasmuch as the long is sometimes divided into two breves and at other times into three or four, which they call "running notes"

[26] Thus, perhaps, by *fractio modi*:

Hammond states (HS, 94) that if the long is divided the result is: . But in the initial sentence of the paragraph Odington speaks of the division of the long into two breves, not of the imperfecting of the long. However, neither of the other two interpretations of this passage is quite satisfactory either (see Sanders, p. 260-61; Dittmer, art. cit., pp. 47 f.). The first sentence of the paragraph is certainly garbled, and it is possible that the remainder is also not as Odington wrote it. Still, Hammond and Sanders are probably right in maintaining that Odington is talking here, as before, about differences of *notation*, not differences of *system*.

[27] "...admixtis pausis diversis." Sanders (p. 271) takes the phrase to mean an indiscriminate use of rest values. Whether it does or not, it seems, in the context, to indicate something typical of the notation of cantilenas, and consequently Sanders deplores the fact that what he assumes to be a promise on Odington's part to discuss that subject later ("...sicut patet posterius in cantilenis") is never fulfilled. However, "sicut patet posterius in cantilenis" may simply refer to some of Odington's own examples in the later *capitula* of part vi as showing how rests appear typically in cantilenas. Certainly many of those examples, as they are found in the manuscript, exhibit an indiscriminate use of rests as well as an "admixture of the different rests." Unfortunately the differentiation of rest values is so uncertain in the manuscript throughout part vi that it is impossible to come to any conclusion about the practice of notating rests in cantilenas from the examples thereof.

(*currentes*). On the other hand, when they write single notes, they use the signs for the breve and semibreve mentioned already, namely: 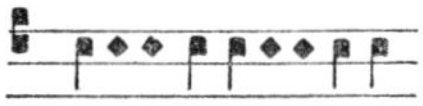. Still others use longs, breves, and semibreves, and rests in these modes according to the system I myself employ but divide the long into only two breves with a value of two *tempora*, and the breve into two semibreves, or occasionally into three. Then the rest for a long occupies two spaces, for a breve, one.

Ligature is not used in the fifth mode because it consists entirely of longs. Occasionally, however, a ligature is found in certain tenors,[28] but then there is no problem.

Ligatures in the sixth mode have propriety or opposite propriety and are without perfection, thus: 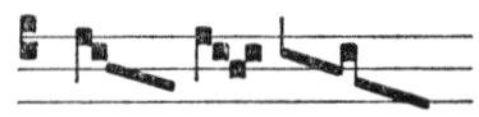. And regardless of how many notes there may be, they can all be bound in ligature unless separated by a rest.

Others proceed by binary, ternary, or quaternary ligature in this mode, guided by nothing but caprice; and they have no sign for the semibreve but change rather to another mode, thus:[29] 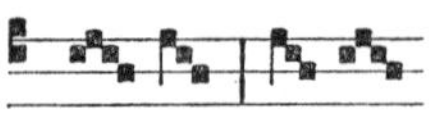. Still others notate this mode with propriety and perfection, plicated, thus: 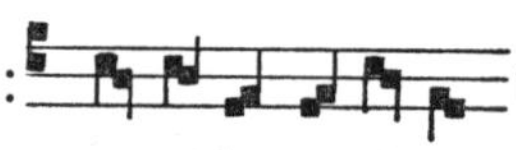 taking the plica for a breve. But this is second mode.[30] It is clear then that the method of notation which I have presented above is the least ambiguous and the one to be preferred.

Types of part-music

There is one type of part-music in which one is concerned

[28] Cf. Franco, HM, p. 247; Strunk, p. 151.

[29] Possibly: 

.

[30] I.e., the *fractiones* of mode 2 produced by the plicas result in mode 6 (cf. Apel, pp. 235-6). Again, Odington condemns an older practice.

purely with the fitting-together of pitches (*cohaerentia vocum*), having no definite time values, and this is called *pure organum*. It is the oldest kind and consists of only two parts. Then, there is another type in which attention is paid to the proper relations (*consonantia*) of time values as well as of pitches. It may be in two, three, or four parts, and is called *discant*, that is, music in at least two parts. But in fact [pure] organum sometimes has one part, sometimes two, because the tenor is occasionally silent while awaiting a consonance.

Moreover, there are several types of discant. For example, if all voices repeat the same thing in succession, the piece is called a *rondellus*, that is, moving in a circle or rotating, and it may be with or without text. But if the voices, rather than repeating the same melody, all proceed with their own individual parts, the piece becomes a *conductus*, that is, several melodies *conducing* to a good effect. There is still another type, which moves by binary ligature like the second mode, only faster and with an unmeasured long at the beginning; and it is called *copula*, a name deriving from the manner of its notation. A second kind of *copula* is written in separate notes, slower than the sixth mode, and is named according to the principle of opposites, i.e., from the fact that its notes are not ligated. Another type [of discant] is concerned with the rhythmic matching of notes and text, as well as with harmony, and it is called *motet*, meaning the motion of a short melody. In another kind of discant, which may or may not have a text, one part rests while another sings, and vice versa. A piece of this sort is appropriately called a *truncation* after its character. It is also referred to as *hocket*.

On the composition of organum [part-music], and of pure organum first

There are certain requirements that apply to the composition of all kinds of part-music, as, for example, that the consonant intervals predominate. And in this connection it should be noted that no breve placed before a long is faulted, even if it makes a discord. Dissonance is also permitted in *moteti colorati* [i.e., motets employing a reiterated rhythmic and/or melodic pattern] when some part of the melody is repeated over the given tenor, as in the following.[31]

Another general requirement is that the individual voices not exceed the range of the trope, that is, a tenth — or an eleventh with the [addition of a] semitone — reckoned ascending or descending from the final.

Pure organum is composed this way: One phrase, or two or three, is selected from some plainchant and arranged as a tenor; and the superius moves with it in consonances and concordant dissonances.[32] There may be any number of the latter but the superius begins at the octave, fifth, or fourth

[31] The example consists of the tenor and duplum of Mo 5, 108 (Y. Rokseth, Polyphonies du XIIIe Siècle, Paris, 1936; Vol. II, No. 108) with the motetus *De penetractoribus* substituted for *Vetus vaticinium*. See HS, pp. 100-101; WO, p. 132.

[32] "...concordant dissonances": *concordes discordias*. The intervals so classified are listed by Odington in part ii, cap. 16: minor third, major third, major sixth, minor tenth, major tenth, and the eleventh.

above the tenor and ends at the octave, fifth, or unison. And it should be sung softly and sensitively, a descent [in *currentes*] quickly and evenly, and the tenor held *tremulo*[33] even when it makes a dissonance.[34]

The rondellus

Rondelli are to be composed as follows: Think up the most beautiful melody possible and put it in one of the above-mentioned modes, either with or without text, and let this melody be repeated by each voice in turn, accompanied by two or three other melodies harmonizing with it in such a way that if the first ascends the second or third descends, not all ascending or descending at the same time, unless it happens that they can produce a more beautiful effect by so doing. Then let the melody of each part be repeated by all the others one by one, thus:

[33] "...tenor autem tremule teneatur et cum discordo offendit." Cf. Guido Aretinus, *Micrologus*, ed. Jos. Smits van Waesberghe (American Institute of Musicology, 1955), pp. 163-4; Engelbert of Admont, *De musica*, in *Scriptores ecclesiastici de musica*, ed. Martin Gerbert (Typis San-Blasianis, 1784), II, 319b & 366b.

[34] The example appears to illustrate so-called "duplum notation" (see, e.g., Apel, pp. 267-271). The transcription is made accordingly.

* The *plica* in the original is ignored here.

** Ms: 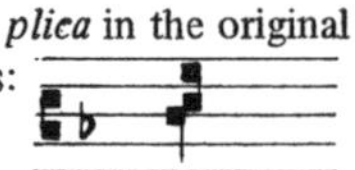

The conductus

Conducti are composed of several melodies of good quality, either known or newly composed, and in various modes, with repeated notes, and either in the same *tonus* or in different *toni*, thus:[35]

* Ms: 

The copula

A ligated copula is to be written either on a single phrase or on more than one, like organum; but it may be in three parts. It begins with an unmeasured long and proceeds by binary ligature in the manner shown here:

[35] The *duplex longa* in the lowest part of the example that follows would produce:  as the last unit in that part. This is rhythmically satisfactory but harmonically not.

* Ms: 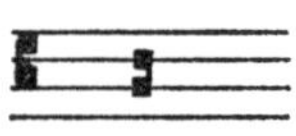.

Or with this tenor: 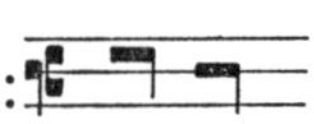  . But if the initial long has the sign of perfection, thus: 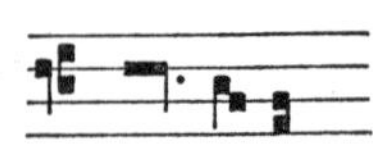  then the piece is in the second mode.

The unligated copula is written the same way only in separate notes, as the following shows:

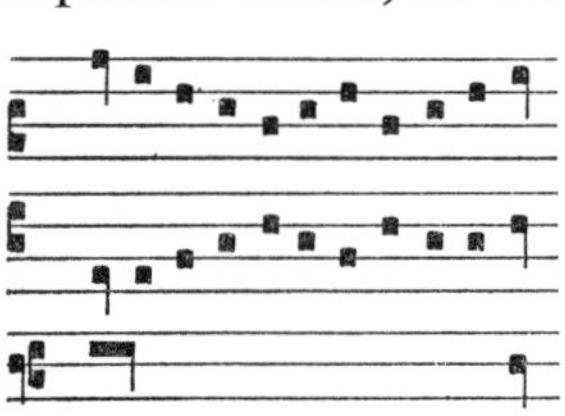

This type [of discant], moreover, whether in ligatures or in single notes, is always placed at the ends of sections unless all parts can properly rest.

The motet

Motets are composed with text and in any of the modes. For the tenor, one takes a well-known melody, suitable for setting, and adapts it to a particular mode. The middle part can be in the same mode or another, as befits the tenor. Thus, the fifth mode can be a tenor for anything else except a middle part set in the sixth mode. The first mode will combine with the sixth and so will the second. The third and fourth will combine with the second mode. But a middle part in the sixth mode requires a tenor in the sixth, though exceptions are sometimes found. And the middle part should receive particular attention, so that it is beautiful in itself. The third part is often written in the sixth mode, although every part can be written in any one of the modes. And one must also see to it that the notes of the discant adapt properly to the syllables of the text, as here:[36]

[36] For sources and history of this motet see HS, pp. 99-100; WO, p. 135. Odington's version of the triplum may be compared with that of Robert of Handlo (CS, I, 402a):

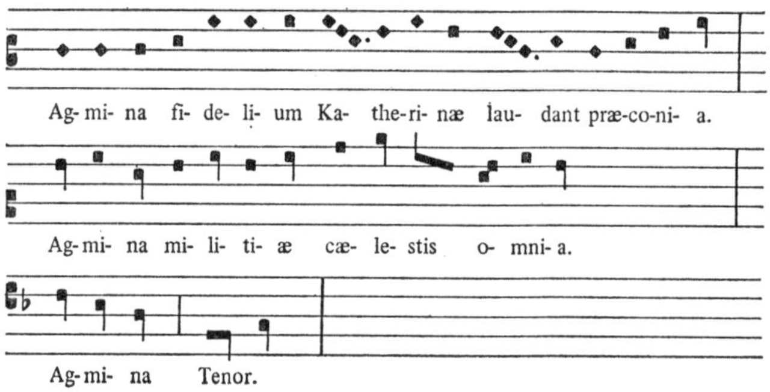

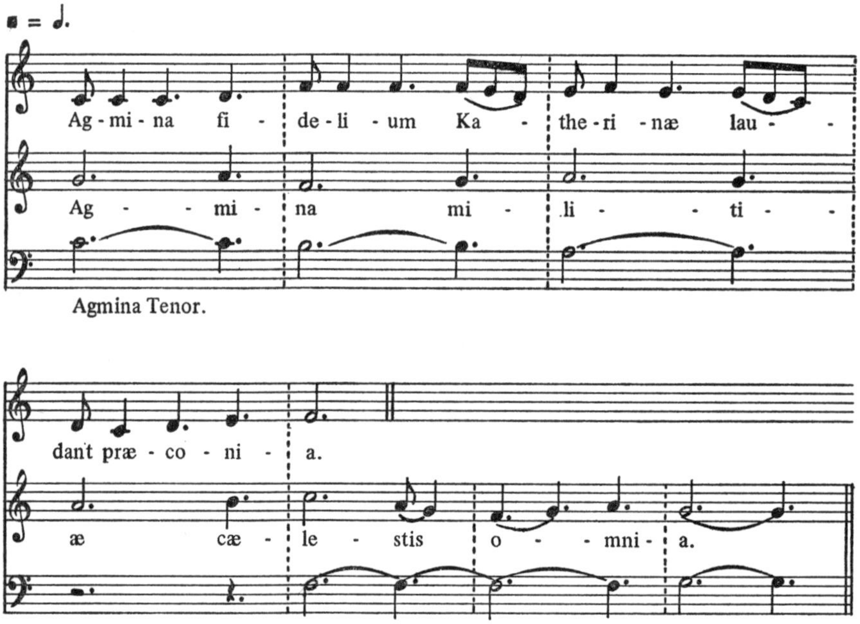

The hocket

This truncation is composed either on an invented or on a given tenor, and in such a way that one part is always silent while the other is singing; or, if it is in three parts, this way: two sing while a third is silent. And it is written in all modes, although everyone who mentions it says it is in the third mode.

In the first mode, as follows:[37]

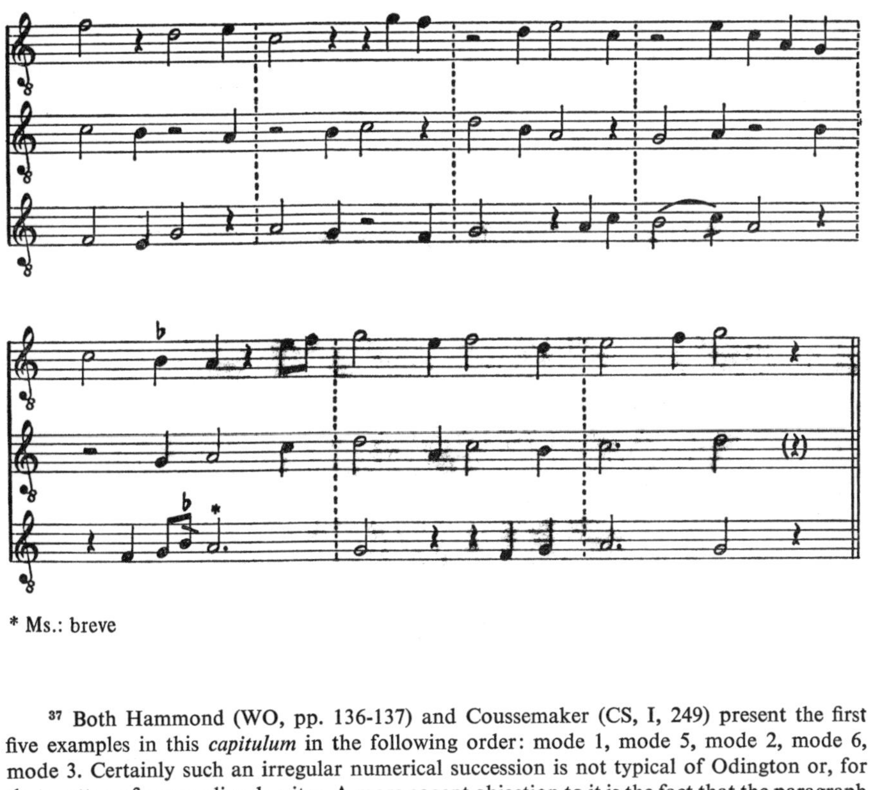

* Ms.: breve

[37] Both Hammond (WO, pp. 136-137) and Coussemaker (CS, I, 249) present the first five examples in this *capitulum* in the following order: mode 1, mode 5, mode 2, mode 6, mode 3. Certainly such an irregular numerical succession is not typical of Odington or, for that matter, of any medieval writer. A more cogent objection to it is the fact that the paragraph that follows, though purporting to refer to the hocket last quoted ("accidit autem dubitatio in hoquetis istius modi ..."), clearly does not, with this arrangement, because the remarks made therein are not relevant to *fractiones* and *divisiones modi* in mode 3.

In the codex the examples in question stand on the page (fol. 35v) approximately this way:

mode 1   mode 2   mode 3
mode 5   mode 6

Thus, if one simply reads across instead of down, the order, by numerical identification of modes, is normal, and the paragraph that follows then comes directly after the hocket in mode 6, to which it can be made to apply.

In the second mode as shown here:

* Ms: 

In the third, thus:[38] And the second is similar to the fourth, as the following shows:[39]

[38] A slightly different version of the hocket in third mode appears in the Bamberg Codex (P. Aubry, *Cent Motets du XIIIe siècle*, Paris, 1908, Vol. II, no. 104). It will be noticed that the two-space rest for the *recta brevis* is retained from the older source.

[39] This sentence as it stands is not applicable to any of the examples. However, if "secundus" is presumed to be a mistake for "tertius," the remark can be taken to refer to the next following hocket, which is made readable in fourth mode as readily as in third by its *extentiones* and *fractiones modi*:  . This interpretation is at least consonant with what appears to be the purpose of the sentence, namely to explain why hocket in mode 4 is not illustrated by a separate example.

* Ms: ■

And in the fifth mode it is written thus:

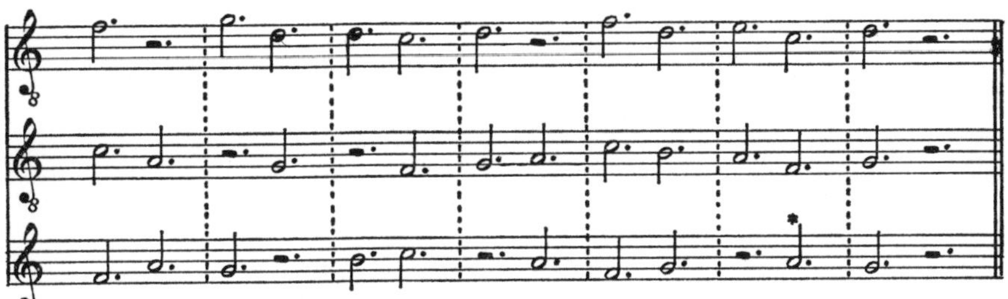

* Ms: *duplex longa*

In the sixth mode thus:

* Ms: E♭

But an ambiguity occurs in hockets of this mode when the breve is divided into three semibreves because the semibreve rest has the same form as the sign of division, and the divisions have to be indicated. However, I want to conform to common practice in such matters, and so a little circle may be placed over the *minutae*[40] as a sign of division, thus:

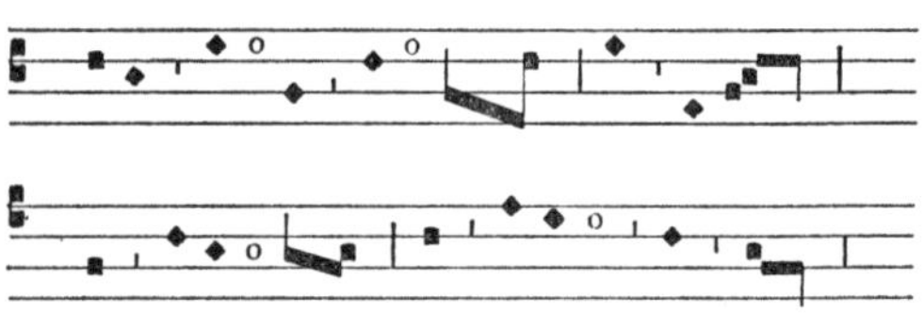

And any of the above types of discant can also be written in four or more parts if one likes, and the same rules apply to those in four parts as to those in three.

There is another kind of hocket, called "simple," which is in only two parts; and it is written on known cantus of good quality in such a way that as one part takes one thing the other

[40] *Minuta* is used here, evidently, as synonymous with semibreve, not as previously defined (vi, 1).

rests, each following the other in turn and dividing up the notes, thus:[41]

Another of the sort is shown here:

[41] It is quite impossible to make musical sense of the hocket that follows as it is notated in the manuscript. The transcription is based on the fewest notational changes necessary to produce a musically acceptable version compatible with Odington's designation "simple hocket," where that phrase is taken to mean a piece consisting essentially of a single melodic line divided between two parts. This interpretation of *simplex* is consistent with its regular meaning, "monophonic" (as, e.g., in the first sentence of part vi) and seems preferable to referring it to the reduction in the number of voice parts from three, in the previous example, to two here.

On the [proper] manner of singing [pure organum]

Let him who is to sing the higher part begin, and in such a way as to suffice for a copula, using that note which is held a long time. Let all the others then succeed to it, singing clearly and evenly according to the common measure of the tempora, softly, but listening: and let them drop out altogether after the penultimate note has been produced. There are other refinements of [organal] singing, however, which cannot be conveyed in words but only by means of a well-trained voice.

Now, let this suffice for a survey of the discipline of music, one which will be the more widely accepted in proportion as it is consonant with the teachings of others. And [so] let no one carp, saying: he repeats what others have said, for this I readily admit. Let me rather be excused if I have failed in any way, and let it be accepted that I offer nothing new seeing that my purpose throughout has been to gather together the various statements of former writers, not to produce a satiety by providing further, new variety.